YOU

Mental help

DANIEL.

THE FALL AND RISE

SHAUN MARSHALL

Copyrights © 2025 by SHAUN MARSHALL

All Rights Reserved

No part of this book may be reproduced or transmitted in any form or by any means, electronic or mechanical, including photocopying, recording, or by any information storage and retrieval system without the written permission of the author, except where permitted by law.

This book is dedicated to all our brothers out there who are still searching.

The inspiration for this book came from the story:

"Don't Let the Light Go Out"

ACKNOWLEDGEMENTS

This book was written with the help of a good friend.

Trish McGowan.

Thank you

TABLE OF CONTENTS

Foreword 1

Chapter 1: Synchronicity and the Negative Loop! 3

Chapter 2: The Unspoken Divide! 5

Chapter 3: Relationships, Breakdowns,
and Blame 8

Chapter 4: Why This Story Matters 10

Chapter 5: Falling Down! 11

Chapter 6: Men at Work 15

Chapter 7: Silence is Not Golden! 19

Chapter 8: The Job! 22

Chapter 9: The Men-Only Club 26

Chapter 10: Just a Little Help, Please! 29

Chapter 11: Still, I Rise 32

Chapter 12: A Faithful Friend 37

Chapter 13: Stepping Out 40

Chapter 14: Happy Endings 44

Chapter 15: Think Like a Woman, Be
Like a Man 49

Chapter 16: Is this You? 51

Chapter 17: Tiring and Frightening! 52

Chapter 18: You and Your Vision 53

Chapter 19: Turn It Around! 56

Chapter 20: Shout It Out Loud 57

Some Positive Thoughts 58

    Alone.. 58

    Blessed... 58

    Power 59

    Strength 59

    Trust the Plan... 60

    A Reminder for You 60

About the Author 61

Other Books By This Author: 63

FOREWORD

This is a *fictional* story about a man named Daniel—his fall and, ultimately, his rise.

Daniel is not just one man. He could be any one of thousands or millions of middle-aged men across the country and even the world.

So, it could be about *you.*

Daniel represents a quiet, often invisible demographic: men who are struggling, silently and without fanfare, with mental health, identity, relationship issues, and the pressures of modern life.

This is not a *factual* account nor a clinical study.

What follows is a deeply personal reflection—a blend of lived experience, observations, and personal insights.

It is **not** written by a guru or a self-help expert.

I am just someone who's lived through his own ***chaos***, made plenty of mistakes, and slowly found ways to cope with my so-called '*special superpowers*'—in my case, ADHD.

If this helps you in any way, it has been worth writing.

It's all about *you!* It's all about *us!*

I have tried to keep it simple, readable, and honest—something I hope real people can connect with.

I am a ladies' hairdresser by trade. In that role, I have had the rare privilege of seeing into people's lives in the way most never do.

Over the years. I have heard it all—the heartbreaks, the dreams, the regrets, the laughter, and the pain.

I have been there for weddings and divorces. The new relationships, hospital visits, break ups, and reconcileiations—even styling hair in the hospital in their final days, always styling hair with a kind smile and, hopefully, humility.

Hairdressers often end up being part therapist, part confidant, but always humble.

So, I've written this story with all of that in mind. My own journey and my observations, mixed with the conversations I have had over the years behind the chair, have shaped the story you are about to read.

It is a portrait of modern manhood.

It is aimed at men in their late forties and beyond through the eyes of someone who's listened and lived it himself.

CHAPTER 1:
SYNCHRONICITY AND THE NEGATIVE LOOP!

Let us talk about *synchronicity*—a beautiful word for a strange, almost mystical phenomenon: "The simultaneous occurrence of events which appear meaningfully related but have no discernible causal connection."

Have you ever noticed that once you start thinking about a certain type of car, you see it everywhere?

Or if you have broken your arm, you suddenly spot slings and plasters on everyone else, too. When a woman is pregnant, every other woman seems to be as well. That is not magic, I think it's a type of mindset—synchronicity.

In Daniel's story, synchronicity is a metaphor for how easily we can all get stuck in a negative loop. When you are spiralling downward, you begin to see the world through that filter. Everything confirms your fears: your self-doubt, your sadness. And if social media has done anything, it's made that spiral faster and darker.

Every scroll reminds us of what we are *not*—not rich enough, not successful enough, not 'living our best life.' It is all so negative.

Have you also noticed that when you're sad, all you can hear are sad songs? But when you're happy, you're singing and jumping around to 'Dua Lipa?'

That is your mindset at that moment.

If you can shift your mindset, even slightly, everything can and will start to change. Change your thoughts, and *you* slowly begin to change your actions. Change your actions, and you might just change your life.

CHAPTER 2:
THE UNSPOKEN DIVIDE!

In this story, I focus mostly on men's experiences. Not because women do not suffer, they do—often more deeply than men—but because their way of coping with their suffering can often look different to us. When life is turned upside down for women, in my experience, women tend to somehow manage and carry on.

Maybe it's because they've had no choice.

They are usually the ones still feeding the kids, getting them to school, planning meals, and keeping routines. The list is almost endless.

Women tend to build social circles more naturally.

Talk to each other and support one another. They meet up, go to fitness classes, and talk openly about emotions. Talk about health and their relationships. Nothing is off limits in a proper women's chat.

They are often the planners. The emotional glue in families, the *connectors*—they make things happen.

Men? We struggle. We isolate. We retreat into ourselves, and we often play the blame game.

There is still a stubborn stigma attached to older men not showing any vulnerability. It's almost an ingrained belief that any kind of vulnerability is seen as a weakness.

We still, in some regards, have that 'macho' image to maintain. We do not talk. We do not want to appear weak. We lose ourselves in work, in silence, in drink, in avoidance. Most middle-aged men I know might have one or two proper friends, if any. They may have plenty of 'mates,' guys they'll watch the match and have a pint with. But *real* friendships, the soul-baring type? It's a rare thing.

We avoid check-ups. We avoid therapy. We avoid facing what is going on, unfortunately, until we're forced.

The most common mental health struggles for men, like anxiety, panic attacks, ADHD, depression, loneliness, and OCD, are kept hidden, buried under banter, bravado, or a stiff upper lip.

Getting men to discuss general mental health issues, let alone *their* own personal struggles, is virtually impossible. Thankfully, younger men are beginning to break that mould. They are talking more.

But even then, these younger guys often just talk with each other. The idea of reaching out to *professionals* for help or advice may not occur to them until they see it as a last resort.

So, what of older men? They haven't yet got the hang of reaching out for help. We are often afraid of being judged for saying the wrong thing. Afraid of showing vulnerability and being perceived as weak.

Take modern dating, for example. Forget it. It's a minefield.

Even that is carried out on a 'phone app' these days. Very little human interaction. Just swiping through endless pictures. Not so much face-to-face.

Approaching a woman today can feel like walking a tightrope. Constant worries about being misunderstood, labelled, unfairly typecast, or outright rejected.

Men are often unsure what the 'rules' are these days. What used to be seen as charming—opening a door, offering to pay for dinner, etc—these things can now sometimes be met with suspicion.

Women today can be fiercely independent, capable, and have their own careers. Most want to be treated as equals, not as objects, and quite rightly so.

But all of this can leave a lot of older men feeling confused, adrift, disconnected. They don't know what the rules are.

CHAPTER 3:
RELATIONSHIPS, BREAKDOWNS, AND BLAME

When relationships break down, men tend to spiral downward. They often blame the other person. We retreat. We nurse the wound in silence and frustration. Women, in my experience, hurt just as much, but they recover differently. They seem stronger, often have a stronger social circle, rebuild, and reconnect. Men find it so much harder to move on. Maybe it's biological. Maybe it's social conditioning. Maybe it's their mindset.

But women seem more able to hold the emotional centre of things, even in chaos. Men often respond by trying to control, with sulking, with avoidance. Fear of loss, insecurity, jealousy—all of it bubbles up and poisons the mind.

In my time as a hairdresser, I have seen it play out a hundred times: men trying to control their partners. Dictating what they wear, who they meet, and what they do. Quite often, it is out of fear of losing the relationship.

And yes, it happens in reverse, too; jealousy is not a gendered trait.

But if a man is already struggling mentally with ADHD, anxiety, or any other inner storm, these issues multiply fast. Everything becomes harder. Everything becomes heavier.

Women are, in my eyes, often smarter in relationships. They seem to see the bigger picture. They are less driven by an ego. Men are more often burdened by the need to achieve, to provide, and appear to be the strong ones. Men, we measure worth in productivity, in results, in status. And when that starts to crumble, we fall hard and feel less of a man.

Many men often work long hours. Travel for work, have dangerous jobs, working away from home. They live under immense pressure, all while, sometimes, quietly breaking apart inside.

And when they come home, they are often too exhausted to engage, too afraid to admit they are struggling. That silence breeds resentment. That silence breaks marriages. That silence may lead to breakdowns at work, at home, and often, ultimately, within themselves.

If there is a health problem lurking in the background, undiagnosed ADHD, depression, or OCD (often perhaps linked to some *past* issues or trauma), it all comes to the surface eventually.

CHAPTER 4:
WHY THIS STORY MATTERS

Daniel's story is fictional, but the feelings are real. The fears, the frustrations, and the downward spiral—they can and are experienced by millions.

But there is a way back.

Not a quick fix. Not a magic cure. But a slow, steady path upward—one shift of *mindset* at a time.

If you are a man who recognises yourself in these pages, know this: you are not weak. You are not broken. *You* are not alone.

And if you are a woman reading this, it may help you understand the vulnerability in the men in your life a little better—fathers, brothers, partners, and sons—and open the door to a conversation that is long overdue.

This is the beginning of Daniel's fall. But stay with him because there's hope on the other side.

CHAPTER 5:
FALLING DOWN!

Daniel had been awake for over an hour, but he had not moved. He was still in bed, the covers twisted around his legs, his back flat against the mattress, his eyes fixed on the ceiling. He'd stared at the same patch of plaster for what felt like a full minute before even realising he was doing it.

The red digital clock on the bedside table blinked at him. 11:47 a.m. Another morning lost, another wasted day.

It didn't really matter too much to Daniel. Most of his days were just the same now, not that much to look forward to. He reached for his phone buried under the covers; the battery was at 6% charge.

One email from his landlord. Subject line read. '*Final warning.*'

He did not bother to open it. He already knew his landlord was chasing him. His rent was overdue again, as were his other utility bills and his gambling debts.

Daniel was renting a flat. It was ridiculously small, with one bedroom, damp, above a shop, no pictures on the wall, and just basic furniture. The wallpaper looked like it had been put up in the 70s, with awful 'orange flowers.' The kitchen had a sink, a wobbly table, and a free-standing cupboard, and the bathroom had the bare minimum. There were no photos of his kids around, not much in the way of any home comforts.

He used to live with his family in a proper house. A three-bedroom home with a garden. A shed full of tools that he pretended to know how to use. A modern kitchen where his son had learned to make pancakes with his mum. The kitchen was always a busy place, full of memories and nice smells. The living room with a huge TV, where his daughter learned to dance with her Nintendo. A nice lawn, friends coming around for occasional summer barbecues, and the car in the drive.

That was all before the divorce. Before everything fell apart. His ex-wife had taken the kids and moved to the coast. Said she needed a clean start and could not cope with him or his issues anymore.

The marriage had completely broken down.

She was looking for a life, love, better schools for the kids, new opportunities, and a space away from him. The love and respect had gone.

Daniel did not fight it. He did not have the strength, the inclination, or the money. He was becoming very depressed and was losing interest in everything. On top of all this, his job was not going well. At 58, he was now renting a cold, drab little flat above a discount chemist shop and trying not to lose the only job he had. His mind was a fog, the same as yesterday, the same as the day before. Depression was setting in and making him start to panic at any little thing.

He stood up slowly and shuffled into the bathroom. On the way, he passed a mirror on the hallway wall; he did not stop to take a look. He did not like what he had become.

His inner voices kept asking him:

How did I get here? Why me?

How can I get out of this situation?

Daniel felt lost. He had always struggled to stay focused, even as a boy. Teachers called him bright but lazy. He was not lazy, his brain just did not work in the way the teachers wanted it to. Everything felt like noise—homework, instructions, conversations. Daniel struggled with them all.

He had been diagnosed with ADHD late in life, the inattentive type. Symptoms can include short attention span, constant fidgeting, and acting without thinking. ADHD is usually categorised in two ways: the inattentive type (difficulty concentrating and focusing) or hyperactivity and impulsiveness.

Many people with ADHD fall between both categories. ADHD is more often diagnosed in boys than girls. Girls are more likely to have symptoms of inattentiveness only and are less likely to show disruptive behaviour.'

Very little was known about ADHD, or any neurodiversity, for that matter, when Daniel was young. A relief to know, but not the solution. Drugs from the doctor helped for a while. Therapy helped a little more, but life kept piling up faster than he could manage or cope.

CHAPTER 6:
MEN AT WORK

Daniel worked for a double-glazing company. He was the logistics manager, responsible for all the stock coming in and out of the warehouse. He had worked there for over 10 years.

New computer systems were coming in. He had never been that great with computers. Work was getting harder now; it was getting more difficult to cope with the speed and the amount of information. He was slower, made small mistakes, struggled to understand the new systems, and often forgot things.

As he got older, life was generally becoming more difficult at work. He had no real friends, had become less confident, and had more panic attacks. He found it difficult to have any fun and relax. He felt he had little to look forward to and had become more stressed.

Sometimes, it was just the feeling that he wasn't accepted or was not good enough. It was an ingrained belief. Sometimes, it was just hard to function in a 'normal' way.

His boss had pulled him aside the week before and told him the company was tightening up, so they were watching his performance. It was polite language. What it meant was, *'Your job and position in the company is on thin ice.'*

He tried harder, but trying wasn't always enough; he had so much stuff running through his mind, particularly the 'divorce.' It was all a jumble, usually full of negative thoughts.

Some mornings, he didn't even make it to work; he just couldn't face it. Panic attacks and his confidence were his nemesis. The fridge was mostly empty: half a bottle of milk, a few eggs (he was not sure they were still in date), and a dried-up piece of cheese. On the table, a takeaway box with a few chips left inside.

He drank a glass of water. There was no coffee or tea in the flat—he had run out the day before. He could not even be bothered to go to the corner shop, let alone the supermarket.

Daniel was aimlessly gazing out of the kitchen window down onto the street. Two teenagers walked past, laughing. One of them tossed a football in the air, completely carefree. They called over to two other friends across the street, asking them to join them in the skate park, not a care in the world.

Daniel moved into the bedroom, leaned on the bedside cabinet and watched them disappear up the street on their bikes. It was the most excitement in his normal, dull day.

He used to have that momentum in his own life. Cutting the grass, washing the car, a family weekend routine. Now, his life was going nowhere. No energy, no drive, no desire—it was all static.

Nowadays, a day out for Daniel was often just sitting alone on a park bench with a few cans of beer. Just aimlessly walking around town, even in the cold, with his head full of constant, aimless negative chatter and despair, feeling worthless, full of self-pity, and very lonely.

He knew where his ex-wife and kids were. She sent photos of the kids now and then with updates on how they were. The boy had started to play the guitar and had got into the local football team. The girl, she was doing very well at gymnastics and was top of her class in maths. They were growing up fast.

He had not seen them in months. He could not afford the trip to go down to them. If he were honest, he did not know how to be around them anymore. He had become quite ashamed of what his life had become and did not want them to see him like this.

At one time, Daniel was a proud husband and father, looking forward to the weekends. Unfortunately, his behaviour and attitude in his marriage and life, in general, got the better of him.

ADHD often made his thoughts very erratic, his behaviour suspect. He had little focus, to the point where he often did not do the things that mattered to the family most, as if he did not care. He did care but often forgot to show it.

He was not sad or angry. He was not sure how he felt, but he knew he could not stay like this for much longer. His negative thoughts came and went.

CHAPTER 7:
SILENCE IS NOT GOLDEN!

There were days like today when he did not speak to another human being. No phone calls, no conversation, no one to ask, "How was your day?"

No one to care what the answer even was! It was so painful to be so alone. Everything seemed pointless.

He sat on the couch, the same one he had for years. It sagged on the left-hand side, his usual spot.

The same pizza takeout box on the coffee table. The same unopened letters. He had thought silence would be easier than the conflict after the divorce. He welcomed it—no more tension, no more arguments, no more trying to explain feelings he could not name.

But silence, he learned, was its own kind of *loud*.

He had not fought for the marriage, not really, when she told him she was done. He just stood there emotionless, watching her pack up her stuff and the kids' clothes and toys.

There was no begging, no breaking down in tears, not even anger; he just let it happen. He was numb inside. He knew she had already made her mind up, and that was it. She was going.

He hadn't seen it at first; he just thought she was tired and stressed. But the truth is *he* made her tired.

His indecisions, silence, lack of motivation, lack of love and care—they all took their toll.

He did not notice the signs of the marriage crumbling. He did but chose to ignore them. He had stopped being someone she could rely on, stopped dreaming, stopped planning, stopped showing any desire for her. He just could not understand himself; his thoughts and feelings were just too chaotic. He let the weight of the world settle on *her* shoulders, and without noticing, she was starting to crumble with the lack of any sort of support from him.

There is nothing sexy about a man who has given up. There is nothing comforting about a man with no fight. Women do not just leave because the love dies; they leave when the effort does.

She asked him once or twice over the years, "Do you still want this life?" or "Do you still want us?"

He said something vague, something like, "Of course I do."

But he had not shown any emotions in months. Not in the ways that matter, not with any purpose. When he came home from work, he was usually tired. He just checked out, turned on the TV, and gave the bare minimum to the family or home. She carried the rest: the house, the kids' birthdays, the emotions, and the dreams. Eventually, and understandably, she left with the kids. She needed a future.

Daniel offered nothing; he was empty. His mental issues were at their peak. Depression, low self-worth, and losing all focus were now his only thoughts. A big problem.

He stood by the kitchen window, making instant noodles for his dinner. Two women were chatting outside the chemist; he couldn't hear what they were saying. They were both carrying shopping bags, laughing and joking. One touched the other on the arm, a small gesture, just a small connection.

No one touched his arm anymore. No one laughed with him. He could not even blame his ex-wife. It was all down to his behaviour.

He had become a man with no confidence, no direction, no passion, and, in his mind, no worth.

In truth, he wanted more, too, but wanting was not enough. He had not acted on it.

He let the years pass, waiting for something to change on its own, and of course, it never did.

That was the day he realised the silence was not punishment; it was a mirror of himself. Finally, it was time to take a good, hard look at himself.

CHAPTER 8:
THE JOB!

It was barely 1 p.m. He was already half drunk. An email sat unopened in his inbox. It was from his manager.

Last week, his manager called him into the office, had him sit down, and smiled politely. He explained that with the downturn in sales, the company was going to slim down the business and scale back staff and business hours. His hours would be changing. He was going to be put on part-time hours. It was nothing personal.

Nothing personal!

He would have his hours dropped to barely part-time. The company was only giving him 2 weeks' notice. In just four weeks, he would be part-time.

He knew he could not live with this little amount of money coming in. He had debts to pay, rent, etc. With no benefits, no security, and little savings, he had no chance of turning it around any time soon.

The company was going to streamline the factory, making it more efficient, including updating all the computer systems.

They would be keeping the younger guys because they were more '*tech*' savvy, faster, hungry, understood the new software, and, of course, were cheaper to employ.

Daniel was fifty-eight years old, slower, often distracted, and at times, becoming very forgetful and unreliable.

He had become expendable, even at work.

He had not told anyone—*what was he going to say?*

He started looking for job vacancies for a similar job. Most positions needed a higher qualification. It turned out he did not have the right qualifications; his were all out of date. He had never bothered with retraining.

He started looking at the government websites to look for any financial help or benefits if any were available. It was a struggle to make any sense of the forms. With ADHD, filling in a form was not his strength. His brain turned administrative tasks into puzzles with missing pieces.

The inner voices were loud again.

You've blown it again.

You're not good enough; you gave up.

She was right to leave you.

You're going to die alone in this shitty flat with no job and nothing to be proud of.

On the few occasions that he left his flat, it was to get bread, milk, or booze. He had started to drink a ***lot***. With too much alcohol and poor eating habits, he had become a miserable sod.

Drinking was becoming his way of dulling the feeling of being worthless and feeling unseen. Or that was his excuse anyway.

He was on a massive downward spiral, being so very lonely, and with little support, he was full of self-pity. He had hit an all-time low. His thoughts were becoming very dark. He was losing the will to live, but he was not going that road yet!

He had choices to make, but his brain gave him so many options, so many voices, that he did not know what direction to take. It felt crippling.

Monday morning came.

He was called straight into the office. Two of the big bosses were there waiting, not looking particularly cheerful.

His part-time job had quickly become no job at all! Daniel was ***fired***! He had been sacked for coming to work under the influence of alcohol. Something similar had happened before a few years ago, but then, he only got a severe warning. This time, it was with immediate effect. The new management had little sympathy for him and would not stand for his behaviour any longer.

He was now at rock bottom. Daniel went home distraught. For the first time in a long time, he stood in front of the mirror and had a good, long, hard look at himself and did not try to *lie* anymore.

It was time. If Daniel did not take the drastic measures he needed to take to find something to bring him back from the brink, he would be homeless.

How could he turn this around? How could he fill his day? How could he survive with no job?

He was aware of all the men he saw in town just hanging around, often in the freezing cold, damp, murky weather, with nothing to do. No hope, aimless, and looking lost.

Some of the men were visibly on something *spicy* and he could see some had mental issues going on.

He knew he was only one step away; this could be him next. Something had to happen fast.

Suicide was constantly on his mind. It had always been there in his head, a small whisper. With every issue, every problem, it became louder.

Was that his way out?

Where to do it! How to do it?

Christ! He was even making a plan!

He had to do something to change his world.

CHAPTER 9:
THE MEN-ONLY CLUB

Daniel pondered the idea of joining a club to get out and meet people, but feeling so lost and depressed, it was little more than a ponderance.

He did not need a club, but where else could he meet people? He needed to find himself again, along with a job, a purpose, and, if he was lucky, some happiness.

He had seen the posters. Local meet-ups for men; a model train club, bird watching, walking groups, art groups, pub quiz teams, all well-meaning, all harmless, but none of it was of any interest to him. None of them got him excited.

A lack of hobbies was not why he was alone. He could buy a jigsaw puzzle or join a fishing group if that was all it took, but it was not.

It was not about staying busy, it was about having a purpose, about feeling alive again, feeling wanted and understood. Being seen!

He wanted a club that gave him back his confidence with a mixture of the sexes, not a boring men-only club.

What's actually missing in a men's club?

For me, it's the presence of *women*.

Not eight guys in the community hall, bantering about sport, the weather, and bloody politics or their sore joints.

It's not because they are not welcoming and friendly—some were very funny—it just does not feel like a real environment.

I know some men do not want women around, so they can be laddish, pretending to still be 'jack the lads' and tell inappropriate jokes, moan about their partner, or maybe they just want to be by themselves; nothing wrong with that. But to me, there is just no *warmth*, just doing!

I feel that real connections are not found in hobbies but in the presence, purpose, and sometimes, simply the company of women.

In my eyes, women tend to be kinder.

Daniel needed a place where there were some women. Women's energy, women's voice, their encouragement, their presence, their kindness. Not for sex, not for romance, just that softness that men don't often know how to give each other.

Daniel tried a men's club, then left, feeling more alone than when he had arrived. What he needed was not noise. It was not banter or trivia; it was space—*to be seen, to talk without performing, to be still without disappearing.*

If he were honest, he missed the way a woman could look at you and just 'know.' Know you were tired, know you were shrinking inside, know something was off even when you smiled. No agenda.

Women have that *sixth* sense. I think they ask better questions and wait for genuine answers. They give you permission to show your feelings and emotions. They have a gentleness.

Daniel did not want to sit in a pub every night; he just wanted someone with him who understood that you can feel empty and full of hope at the same time. The world did not seem to offer much to men like him at his age. Divorced, broke, and sober one day but not the next.

Just trying to hold on. Just trying to belong.

CHAPTER 10:
JUST A LITTLE HELP, PLEASE!

There is a lot of help available out there. If only some men weren't too stubborn, too shy, and too embarrassed to even ask for help. If you have that 'lone wolf' energy, it's often not a personality trait but a trauma response born from a life experience. Starting to heal from your issues requires connections, not isolation.

I have listed some charities that do amazing work:

Movember:

This is one of the leading charities trying to change the face of men's health on a global scale. It focuses on men's mental health, suicide prevention, prostate cancer, testicular cancer, and relationship issues.

Calm:

'Calm' has been helping prevent suicide since 2005. I highly recommend their monthly newsletter.

Headupguys:

The world's leading men's mental health resource. What started as a simple survey in a doctor's waiting room became the catalyst for creating this amazing group.

***

We know men are more likely to die by suicide than women. For many men, opening up about their thoughts and feelings can be difficult and overwhelming.

Movember, Calm and *Headupguys* are all phenomenal charities with worldwide reach. Their platforms are readily available to help men with mental health issues, and like other charities, are making a significant impact. Sadly, despite this, the suicide rate in young and older men is rising at a very rapid rate.

I have put together a list of resources to help support men's mental health at the end of this book.

It seems that when men get to the stage where life becomes overwhelming, it is much more difficult for them to climb out of it, so many do not—*or cannot.* Unfortunately, some end up on the streets with all sorts of mental health issues or worse.

With a family breakdown, often it's women who tend to keep the family home, particularly and understandably, when children are involved. Men tend to have to start finding places to live. Today, renting can be extremely expensive, and affordable flats or apartments are in very short supply.

Before you slam the book shut in rage at that last statement, I admit I am generalising—but you must agree, men seem not to have it so easy.

Men are often placed at the bottom of any housing lists, benefits can be harder or impossible to obtain, it can be quite difficult to find a meaningful job at a certain age, and with little or no social circle, life can be very brutal.

A nasty fact: "Every 41 seconds, the world loses another to mental illness."

CHAPTER 11:
STILL, I RISE

Daniel had seen an advertisement about men's wellness. At first, it felt pointless. He was a complete nonbeliever, but it was strongly recommended to try affirmations to try to build positive thoughts in his head. What did he have to lose?

Over the weeks, he had stopped drinking quite as much. He felt a determination to push through to a more positive mindset. Affirmations are said to be a useful tool to fill your head with positive thoughts instead of the negativity you have been experiencing. He felt ridiculous saying the words out loud but was prepared to give it a go.

"I am good enough."

"I am going to have the best day of my life today."

"I am positive, and I reject negativity."

"I am loved and worthy of love."

"I am positive. I can achieve anything I put my mind to."

The list went on and on.

Eventually, after many weeks of trying to feel better about himself each morning, he found a guy on YouTube. He started with affirmations. The program was called *'I Am—Morning Affirmations for Positive Thinking.'*

The words 'I am' being the keywords.

Daniel started to feel a shift; he slowly became calmer in his mind, less panicked, and had more positive voices in his head. He started to have more belief. More importantly, he found himself saying the words like he meant them, *really* meant them. He slowly began to believe he had hope.

It's not just about the words. It's about finding help and understanding. It's about giving yourself time. It's not giving up on something just because it does not make a difference straight away. Men often look for a quick fix.

He joined the local library and started reading real books, not newspapers or gossip columns of lives that were not his. He was with other people; it was just nice to hear the chatter.

Libraries are much different today than they were when Daniel was a kid. It was all quiet and hushed voices back then. Today, it is completely different. You can get a coffee, watch films, seek advice, and do almost anything. There was even a position vacant section, people to advise on all sorts of things, and help with banking. It was a revelation!

After looking around for a few weeks, he managed to find a volunteer position at a local food bank. He needed something, a purpose. Somewhere to occupy himself and feel valued.

He was a little reluctant at first to work for no wage, but he volunteered and started to work. It was only a few hours a week, just unpacking boxes and greeting people. It gave him the structure he needed and a sense of purpose, and it used up a lot of his time in the day. He felt wanted and enjoyed himself.

No one cared that he did not have any money or was starting over again at his age. They just appreciated all the help they could get. He was not judged.

That is where he met Lena.

Lena also volunteered on the weekends at the food bank. She was in her mid-fifties, had a nice, soft voice and lovely green eyes, and was interesting to talk to. She took Daniel under her wing and showed him how the systems worked and what had to be done at the food bank.

She always had something interesting to say in their conversations. She was easy to be around and simply a nice person.

They talked about insignificant things at first—work stuff, logistics, deliveries, the weather, just banta. She made him feel he had worth again. At the food bank, they all understood he had issues, like some others who worked there, so all were very accommodating to his plight.

Lena had her own issues. She was recovering from an abusive relationship. A husband who took her for granted was violent and generally made her life miserable. She did not discuss this anymore as it was in her past, and she had mostly put it behind her. But sometimes, there was a sadness in her eyes.

One morning, Daniel asked if she wanted to grab a coffee sometime later. He nearly took it back the second he said it, but she smiled and said, "Sure, that would be nice."

They met at a small café in the park. He showed up 10 minutes early and sat by the window, stirring sugar into a coffee he did not really want. He had not been on a date in years; he wasn't even sure if it was a date, just company. He did not really know what he wanted.

She arrived on time, with no makeup—she was just naturally pretty—a warm smile, and a book in her bag. Lena ordered a pot of green tea, a selection of cakes, and another coffee for Daniel.

The conversation started slow. He worried he was talking too much. Then they just found a rhythm and talked about work and old films. She mentioned her kids, neither of them pretending life had been easy for either of them. They did not flirt; they connected.

The experts say we tend to attract people with similar emotional patterns. If you are anxious and clingy, everyone feels it. If you are distant, guarded, or an avoidant type, people feel that, too. Avoidant types can be particularly difficult in any relationship.

Apparently, we seek out what is familiar in our relationships and emotional patterns from our past, even when those patterns actually hurt us emotionally. So, be careful who you bring into your life!

A big part of Daniel's journey is to learn about himself. It is difficult, but if it were easy, we would all be perfect, and we are not, and that is also fine.

Remember, you're good enough as you are.

Daniel had spent years avoiding his own feelings, and somehow, his ex-wife had done the same. They had just danced around each other until there was nothing left.

CHAPTER 12:
A FAITHFUL FRIEND

Lena.

She wasn't flashy. She wasn't loud. But she had a depth, a sincerity. She carried herself like someone who'd had to figure things out the hard way and survived. Her voice was soft but steady, like someone who'd spent years listening before she ever needed to speak, something Daniel struggled with!

Daniel often acted before thinking, and the outcome often hurt people's feelings or did not get the desired effect. Lena lived alone. She had two grown sons who had their own lives and had moved away. She was going to be a very proud grandma soon. The drama with her controlling, abusive ex was becoming a distant memory.

She used to work in the city for a large global finance company but now worked part-time at a local charity shop and volunteered at the food bank on weekends, not for the halo effect, but because it gave her a new structure and clarity and a much calmer, less pressured workplace and lifestyle.

She had a dry wit, a low laugh, and sharp eyes. Very practical and organised. She didn't flatter. She noticed.

She noticed when Daniel was fidgeting, when he talked too much or not enough, and when he ducked the hard questions. She never pushed, but she also didn't let things slide.

"You don't have to impress me," she told him once over coffee. "I already see you."

She was not one for taking bullshit from anyone. The financial world had been a tough place to work.

She had boundaries, too. She didn't want to be needed like a lifeboat. She wanted friendship. Real time. Shared silence. Someone who could sit in the hard moments and not run.

Lena had learned years ago that companionship was only healthy if it let both people breathe. She wasn't looking to rescue anyone. She was looking to walk beside someone who could hold their own and help them get back up.

With Daniel, something about the stillness between them felt right. No pressure. No pretence. Just presence.

But they were both honest about being human, and that was rare. Lena was different. She was not looking for validation or a romantic relationship—not looking for anything. She was just a genuinely nice person, honest and open. She was happy helping Daniel move his life forward and liked him as a person. Lena was enjoying her freedom and relished not to be at the beck and call of someone who did not appreciate her.

Life started to look better again for Daniel. He had found a friend who 'saw' him, who gave him hope again. A little job where people appreciated his efforts. He felt he had found his place. He was more peaceful within himself.

It was less about earning money now; it was more about the connections he was making.

CHAPTER 13:
STEPPING OUT

It wasn't a miracle. It was a slow transformation, even uncomfortable at times, but it was real.

Over the coming months, he managed to get a job with help from Lena. A full-time paying job at the food bank with responsibilities.

He had three volunteers working with him to help fill and stock the shop with the donated food. He was working Wednesdays to Saturdays.

Daniel was on his way, still doing affirmations each morning. The drinking and gambling had stopped. His life was starting to change for the better. However, it took time.

He saw Lena socially once a week at first, then twice a week. It became something quite nice and steady, just two people choosing to show up, no games, no pretence.

Daniel started to live a meaningful life again, building his confidence, cleaning his home, eating properly, and taking care of himself. He had a dream again. He was even managing his ADHD symptoms much better. Life felt richer.

So, to all the men who might have taken the time to read this, you're not alone. Take a leaf from Daniel's story and find a friendly face to connect with. It's a great place to start.

Check out the *Movember*, *Men's sheds, Mind, James'place,* and *Calm* web pages, all offering powerful information and tools to help men with mental health issues.

Find your real friends. Ones that lift you up, not the friends who are always on a downer. Go outside into nature as much as possible. Start talking to yourself with positive, kind words. Try journalling—a diary of your activity, thoughts, and milestones. Journalling is becoming a popular way for both men and women to record their innermost feelings.

Your words are powerful, so make sure they're nice. There is help out there, but you need to be open to the positive and want to find it. When the time is right for you, with your new 'mindset,' you will.

Use every tool you can find. There is a wealth of tools out there now if you have local libraries or access to the Internet. Find something that 'fits' you.

Youtube, hypnosis, affirmations, talking therapy, whatever it takes to get you listening and taking positive steps. For me, it was my few faithful friends who helped me the most by just being there for me as I listened to their advice—reminding me that I was good enough just as I am, making sure I took some sort of action, and actually trying to find ways to help myself.

You find out who your true friends are when you're in a crisis. Find help! I can't stress this enough. Do things with a friend, even if it's simply having a coffee, and try to occupy your mind. Try to do things that make your heart sing.

Park runs, and now park walks, are becoming a massive thing. I notice both men and women love this sport. In my town, it's definitely dominated by men.

Any sport is a terrific way to keep fit and relieve that stress in your mind. Eventually, the negative voices in your head will become quieter. Go out walking—if you have a dog, it's a great place to start, as they always want to go out. If you haven't got a dog, borrow one. The owners will love you, and dogs—they love to walk in any weather at any time.

Speak good words to others, talk to strangers, use positive words to yourself, and become more grateful. Just take a step back and put yourself first in your thoughts. I know it is exceedingly difficult to stop the negative thoughts, but with time, it does get easier—and if the sun is out, it is even better.

I am not saying that the voices ever go away completely, but they become easier to cope with. For me, it's much nicer and easier to do some of these things with someone else. Someone who sees you not for sympathy but for good company.

Also, please remember that if you have had a long period of time with a very poor diet and alcohol, you might *need* extra vitamins and minerals to support your body and mind. I personally would recommend ashwagandha, magnesium, and vitamin B12. They definitely help calm my thoughts. But of course, please check with your doctor before you take any sort of medication, especially iron.

Disregard what others think of you. You can't be what others want you to be. Stop trying to please everyone else. Put yourself first.

Don't watch or listen to the news. It's just depressing and may make you become more anxious and depressed. It takes time and hard work to get yourself together. But remember, you're worth it, and only you can do it.

Say it!

"I am perfect just as I am."

Today, "I am going to be the best version of myself."

"I am grateful."

"I am rich in my heart."

"I am strong."

"I am worthy of love."

CHAPTER 14:
HAPPY ENDINGS

This story is coming to an end.

The words and thoughts within these pages can easily be applied to women. The stresses in life are not gender specific. Stress is part of the human condition generally.

Women are not immune to the harshness of life, its trials and tribulations; they just seem to handle it in a different way from us.

We all know how difficult life can be. The pressure of social media, our expectations, finding love, misunderstandings over the phone, misunderstood texts, instant gratification, and relationships. We all have so much *pressure*. Our brains were not designed to cope with all this information. But this? It's about Daniel's journey. His fall to the depths of depression and his eventual *rise* to glory.

It wasn't easy for him to find out all this stuff about his mind. Why had his behaviour messed up so many chances, opportunities, relationships, and, ultimately, his marriage and career? But now, with a better understanding of himself, he is becoming an all-round better person. If only the issues could have been addressed when he was much younger.

Lena helped show him a different way with *patience* and understanding.

Daniel and Lena have now become good friends, doing stuff together and just hanging out.

Just two people, no agenda, no expectations—just friends.

But what is a *friend*?

Friends help each other get back up! That is what friends do.

Daniel now has a new career he really enjoys. He has found a new direction and feels he has his mojo back.

Eventually, after many, many months of hard work, Daniel became the manager of distribution in his area for five food banks. It is quite a demanding job. It takes up his time and comes with a lot of responsibility, which he thrives on. He's so proud to be really helping other people in the community and giving something back. He likes it that people now *see* him. He has found his self-worth again.

Daniel enjoys meeting people from all levels of society in his work. He feels humbled that he is now in a position to give something back to people who need help. His empathy for their situation is real; he understands what it means to be at rock bottom.

He now has a nice apartment, a place he can call his home. He sees his children every other week and has a much better relationship with his ex-wife. They are now talking properly to each other for the first time in years, which is better for everyone, especially the children.

He has become a better father and has become more proactive in their lives, often taking them out for some weekend activities. His children love seeing their dad smile again. The kids say it is great to have Dad back in their lives again.

Getting the right help for Daniel's mind and mental health issues was all that was needed for him to understand his issues and for someone to make him do something about it. Finding the right help, the *right people.* It is a shame for some of us that it takes us far too long to be honest with ourselves and ask for help.

Daniel is starting to build himself a bright new future. Lena is still working at the food bank. She, too, has increased her working time. She is still working alongside Daniel; she has now become his coordinator. Daniel still needs some support; he's not perfect.

Life is good. Simpler, with fewer distractions and more balance, it's just a nice life. Daniel is becoming the man he could have always been if only he'd had the support, the tools, and the knowledge to help himself.

Lena. Was she his gift from the universe that he so desperately needed? Probably. She saw Daniel with all his failings, insecurities, and faults and gave him the oxygen and time to shine.

He thought she was his guiding light. She had faith in him. Maybe it was just the right time for Daniel.

Remember. *You* are the most important person in your life, in your story. You must start looking for opportunities, start looking after your health, start looking for things that help you become happier, and surround yourself with people who love and care for you. When you're happy with yourself, you will find more happiness and positive things all around.

Today is the best day to start. Stop thinking about it; just do something. Take baby steps.

When I was deeply depressed, I was in a very dark place, and I really couldn't see a way forward. In one of my therapy sessions, I was told to look out for *hearts*! *They're everywhere, apparently*, so the therapist told me.

I couldn't see any. I looked for ages but never saw one. Eventually, after weeks of going to the therapist and many months of looking, I started to see big red ones. Not many to start with, but eventually, I started to see them on the backs of cars, in shop windows, and even on people's clothing.

The point is that it is your mindset. When you are ready, you will start to see life with different eyes and different possibilities. You will, as in my case, begin to see hearts.

As I said before, when we're sad, all we hear are sad songs. When we're happy, we hear the happy tunes. It is your mindset. *Synchronicity*. Call it what you like.

Please remember it can take a long time. It isn't easy, and it can be very, very lonely. With the help of someone like Lena in your life or a good friend, your mindset can and will change.

The world has become a very lonely place, so fast-paced that it's easy to feel more isolated in this uncertain world. Once common standards of decency and respect seem to have worn away, trying to find out where *you* fit in is the most challenging thing, but it's possible if you only stop and take a breath.

CHAPTER 15:
THINK LIKE A WOMAN, BE LIKE A MAN

That may sound like a very strange statement, so please give me a moment to try to explain.

How about trying to stop thinking like a man? Drop that big ego for a moment, and instead, think about what you really want to become. Think about the other people around you and how your actions may affect them.

Think about the bigger picture, your future, your vision, think about your family, become more caring towards yourself, and think about what and who you want to become and how you want to be seen by others. Women do this all the time, even the children think this way.

Give yourself permission to be you, and spend more time on yourself. Do the important things that make you feel! Try to create a small but meaningful support group of friends around you, just like women do.

Become more grateful. Try to get involved in making connections and remember how blessed you are, in fact, how blessed we all are, even when we're in the most despair. It is about *your* journey. Your self-discovery. It's about *YOU*.

So, just for a moment, try to think how women do.

As men, we have a tendency to rush to try and fix things, even things that cannot be fixed. An example of this could be how men often think they can fix a crumbling relationship, even when it is too late.

The male ego often gets in the way, perhaps because of what we think society expects from us.

In my experience, as I have said before, women often tend to look at the whole picture and are kinder to themselves. So, give yourself a chance and try to think differently. *It's just a thought.*

What's the worst that can happen if you give it a try?

CHAPTER 16:
IS THIS YOU?

Five signs men find it hard and difficult to move on due to the impact of past hurt on their mental health.

1. Men's sense of worthiness comes from work or being in a relationship. Even when they get it, it's still sometimes not enough.

2. Often, men struggle with boundaries and often try to keep everyone happy.

3. Men often feel insecure in a relationship due to a fear of abandonment, which only creates anxiety, jealousy, and constant rumination.

4. They often try to avoid conflicts at all costs.

5. They tend to re-watch movies or binge-watch TV shows, scrolling endlessly through social media. It's a way to bring something familiar and predictable into their lives. That's also an ADHD thing.

CHAPTER 17:
TIRING AND FRIGHTENING!

Have you ever felt anxious?

This is what *anxiety* can feel like: trouble sleeping, increased irritability, trouble concentrating, loss of appetite, restlessness, a feeling of being on the edge, and feelings of guilt and shame. It can take all of your confidence.

Having anxiety and depression is like being scared and tired at the same time. You can feel your heart pounding. It's the fear of failure. But no urge to be productive. It's wanting friends but hating to socialise. It's wanting to be alone but not wanting to be lonely.

It's often caring about nothing. It is feeling everything at once, then feeling paralysing numb.

It's often forgetting the important things, forgetting to say thank you, being truly grateful and being present in the moment, but forgetting even something simple like holding your loved one's hand. All these things get forgotten.

Remember, knowledge is power!

CHAPTER 18:
YOU AND YOUR VISION

I have repeated myself a few times in this story. That's because it is so important you take notice of the words. For myself, quite often, I need to hear the same thing many times before it sinks in—before I do anything or believe it might even help me.

So, please, be gentle with yourself. Remember to be grateful for everything you have. Stop taking things for granted; be kind to yourself and others. Be available for yourself.

Remember. It's not always a performance. Men usually think everything is about their performance.

Find your way to accomplish *your* goals.

Take small steps. Be nice to yourself and others.

Remember. Anything and everything is possible if you just put your mind to it.

We all deserve second chances.

Your thoughts become things! Think your dreams into reality. Keep looking for hearts or whatever your thing might be. It is your mindset...*synchronicity*.

I hope this, in some way, will help you with your thoughts. I can only tell you I have been through something similar to this myself, so I know how the despair feels.

I am not an expert on the mind. But I have been through all this. All these suggestions definitely helped me. It was a struggle, and it took time, a lot of time and a lot of soul-searching.

I'm not fully there yet, but I'm much more positive. My mindset is so much better now.

I'm still a work in progress, but with the help of good friends, self-belief, and time, I'm confident I'm on my way. Admitting and understanding that I had issues and needed extra help was the start.

Being open to help from anywhere is a good thing. I have learned that it is not a sign of weakness; it is strength. ADHD and other mental health issues can be your superpower. Use them.

You're different because you were made that way, and that's just fine. Understand and embrace your differences. Celebrate your uniqueness. Good luck on your journey. I wish you all the love and success you deserve.

If you find love in your life, make sure you cherish, respect, and grow it. Don't take it for granted. Try not to let go of it. We are not meant to be alone.

Take responsibility for your actions before you take advice.

I hope this helped *YOU*.

We are good enough!

You are good enough!

CHAPTER 19:
TURN IT AROUND!

If anything in this fictional story feels familiar to you, please know this: *You're not alone. You're not broken. There is help.*

Whether you're dealing with loneliness, depression, ADHD, grief, or just feeling stuck—there are people and organizations that can listen, guide, and support you. No judgement. No shame. Try to find that one special friend.

Asking for help isn't a weakness.

It's the first real act of strength.

The resources listed below exist for a reason. Because many of us have felt exactly what you're feeling now, and they got through it. So can *you*.

Take what you need. Reach out when you're ready.

Below are some resources to help you if you're finding things difficult.

CHAPTER 20:
SHOUT IT OUT LOUD

If you'd like a free, confidential, and anonymous conversation about how you're feeling, you can also text SHOUT at 85258 (only free in the UK) to speak to a trained volunteer today.

Information / helpful places

Movember: Uk.movember.com

Info.us@movember.com

Headupguys: Headupguys.org

Www.mensmindmatter.org

Calm: the calm zone.net

Help living and coping with ADHD

Getinflow.io

Adhdfoundation.org.uk

Mind.org.uk

You can also contact us in the **UK**.

NHS on *111*. The Samaritans on *116123*

It is a *free* call.

SOME POSITIVE THOUGHTS

Alone

A weak person is found in the crowd seeking validation and attention

A strong person is found alone, seeking the higher self and trying to heal themselves.

Blessed

Make it a habit to talk about your blessings and your gratitude more than your burdens.

When you spread positivity, the universe blesses you with even more blessings.

Shut the door that triggers you, no matter how fascinating it is.

Be disciplined about what you let into your life.

Where your focus goes, your energy flows.

Power

The power of the tongue is so real.

Stop saying you're tired, you're broke, or you're depressed all the time.

Start saying you're grateful. Start manifesting personal growth.

Start speaking life into yourself.

Strength

While others were free to grow, you were fighting to survive.

Your mind was learning how to survive while they were learning how to thrive.

That is not your fault.

Those without trauma had a different path.

They could focus on dreams while you focused on making it through each day.

They could plan futures while you were healing.

You're not behind. You're not slow. You were just carrying weights they never had to lift.

Your energy went to survival, while there's went to growth.

You have an inner strength; they might never know.

It might be difficult being you, but keep being you.

Trust the Plan

Sometimes, the universe takes you on a journey you did not know you needed to bring you everything you ever wanted. Trust the plan.

A Reminder for You

Never lose hope. Just when you think it's over, the universe sends a miracle your way.

Keep believing in yourself.

It's all about *YOU.*

ABOUT THE AUTHOR

Shaun is a man with a rare gift of seeing and feeling what others often overlook. A successful businessman, artist, and father, his creativity stems from years in a creative environment, so he sees life slightly differently. His journey was paved with heartbreaks, triumphs, his unshakable faith. He finds meaning in small moments that often go unnoticed. With a belief in second chances, he finds joy in uncovering the positive in every experience and person he meets. His writings always come from his heart and soul, and he never stops believing. For those who have loved and lost, seek healing through his words, and those who are still yet to believe in the power of hope, Shaun's words and thoughts await you.

Shaun Marshall
DREAMSCAPE PHOTOGRAPHY

https://samarshallphotography.picfair.com

OTHER BOOKS BY THIS AUTHOR:

Tails From the Trail

The hilarious chronicles of dog walking and dog walkers. A serious, funny, true-to-life read. If you love your dog, you will recognise this.

Don't Let the Light Go Out

A story of true love, rejection, insecurity, and total loss. A sad but true story of how mental health issues can destroy relationships.

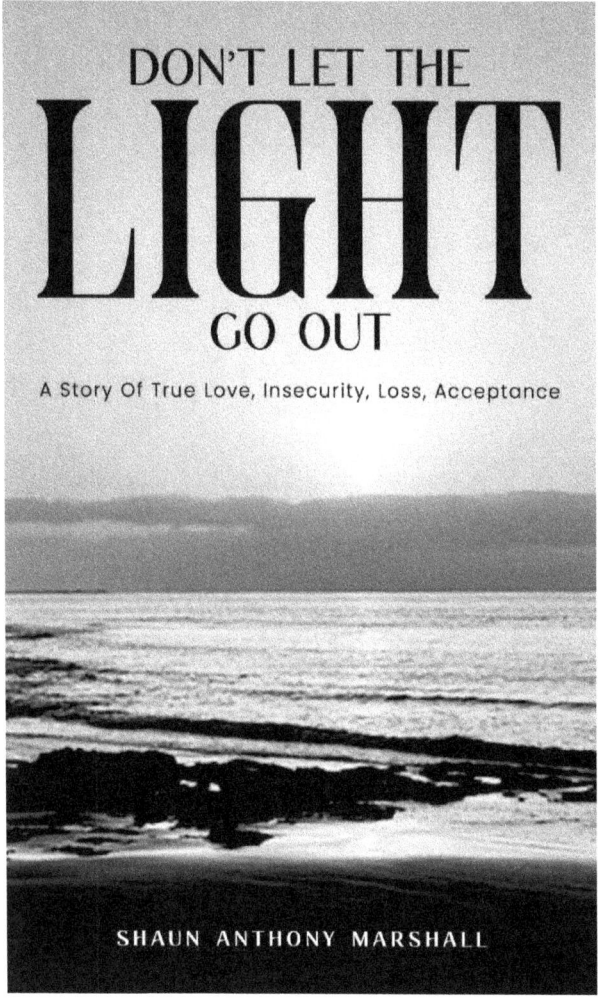

www.ingramcontent.com/pod-product-compliance
Lightning Source LLC
Chambersburg PA
CBHW070313010526
44107CB00004B/321